LANGUAGE ARTS

EXPLORER JUNIOR

How to Write a Poem

by Cecilia Minden
and Kate Roth

INK

CHERRY LAKE
Publishing

Published in the United States of America by Cherry Lake Publishing
Ann Arbor, Michigan
www.cherrylakepublishing.com

Content Adviser: Jeannette Mancilla-Martinez, EdD, Assistant Professor of
Literacy, Language, and Culture, University of Illinois at Chicago

Design and Illustration: The Design Lab

Photo Credits: Page 6, ©Dmitriy Shironosov/Shutterstock, Inc.;
page 10, Denis Pepin/Shutterstock, Inc.; page 11, ©iStockphoto.com/
EVAfotografie; page 16, ©iStockphoto.com/seanfboggs

Library of Congress Cataloging-in-Publication Data
Minden, Cecilia.
  How to write a poem/by Cecilia Minden and Kate Roth.
     p. cm.—(Language arts explorer junior)
  Includes bibliographical references and index.
  ISBN-13: 978-1-60279-995-0 (lib. bdg.)
  ISBN-10: 1-60279-995-4 (lib. bdg.)
  1. Poetry—Authorship—Juvenile literature. I. Roth, Kate. II. Title.
III. Series.
  PN1059.A9M56 2011
  808.1—dc22   2010030066

Cherry Lake Publishing would like to acknowledge the work
of The Partnership for 21st Century Skills. Please visit
www.21stcenturyskills.org for more information.

Printed in the United States of America
Corporate Graphics Inc.
January 2011
CLSP08

Table of Contents

CHAPTER ONE

Poetry

Writing poetry is a way of sharing what we're thinking or how we feel. **Poems** can be short or long.

Some poems **rhyme**. Others do not.

Like music, poems have a **rhythm** or beat. Rhythm is a pattern of beats and sounds. Put your hand on your heart. Can you feel the *da-dum, da-dum* of your heart beating? That is your heart's rhythm.

Would you like to be a **poet**? Here's what you'll need to complete the activities in this book:

- Notebook
- Pen

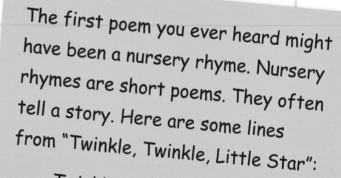

The first poem you ever heard might have been a nursery rhyme. Nursery rhymes are short poems. They often tell a story. Here are some lines from "Twinkle, Twinkle, Little Star":

Twinkle, twinkle, little star
How I wonder what you are!
Up above the world so high
Like a diamond in the sky.

Which words rhyme in this poem?

5

CHAPTER TWO

It Rhymes!

Can't think of words that rhyme? Try asking friends for ideas.

A **couplet** is two lines of poetry that come one after the other. They often rhyme. A couplet can be a short poem. It can also be a **stanza** in a longer poem. Stanzas are groups of lines that make up parts of a poem. Let's write a rhyming couplet.

You can write rhyming couplets about almost anything.

Writing a Couplet

INSTRUCTIONS:

1. Pick a favorite activity to do or place to visit. Write it down in your notebook.
2. Write a list of several words that rhyme with the activity or place.
3. Write a rhyming couplet using some words from your list.
4. Make changes until your poem is just right.
5. Write a title for your poem at the top of the page.

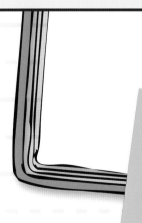

ACTIVITY OR PLACE:
The beach
RHYMING WORDS:
Peach, reach, teach, screech, speech

The Beach

Every summer I go to the beach.
High in the sky the seagulls screech.

SCREEECH!

CHAPTER THREE

Taking Shape

What would you write in a shape poem about football?

Shape poems are poems that take the shape of what you are writing about. For example, a shape poem about a football looks like a football. These poems usually don't rhyme. Let's write a shape poem about hands.

You will need to trace your hand for your hand poem.

Shape Poem

INSTRUCTIONS:
1. In your notebook, write down different things you can do with your hands.
2. Lightly trace your hand on a sheet of paper.
3. Write your poem along the edge of your drawing. Use your list of ideas.
4. Make changes until your poem is just right.
5. Write a title for your poem at the top of the page.

My Handy Hands Can . . .

Pet a cat

Catch a ball

Point to a star

Pick a flower

My Handy Hands Can . . .

CHAPTER FOUR

Making Sense of It

Our senses help us learn about and understand the world. The five senses are taste, touch, smell, hearing, and sight. You use your senses every day. Let's work each of the five senses into a poem.

ACTIVITY

Senses Poem

INSTRUCTIONS:
1. Choose a favorite holiday.
2. Write the holiday at the top of a page in your notebook.
3. Write down things you like about that holiday.
4. Think about which senses you use for each of the things you like. Write about each sense on a different line.
5. Make changes until your poem is just right.
6. Write a title for your poem at the top of the page.

THANKSGIVING IDEAS:
- Yummy smells
- Kitchen full of food
- Tasty pies

I Sense It's Thanksgiving!

I see a kitchen full of food.
I touch vegetables fresh and crisp.
I smell the turkey in the oven.
I taste the pecans while we're baking pies.
I hear my family laughing.
I love Thanksgiving!

This example is a free verse poem. **Free verse** poems don't rhyme or have a set rhythm.

CHAPTER FIVE

Poem on the Side

Bring your notebook wherever you go. You never know when you'll get ideas for poems!

An **acrostic** is like a puzzle. These poems usually do not rhyme. Going down, the first letter of every line spells a word. This word is the subject of the poem. Each line going across describes that subject.

Acrostic Poem

INSTRUCTIONS:
1. Choose someone who is special to you.
2. In your notebook, write a list of things that make this person special.
3. Write the person's name down the left side of the sheet.
4. Write a poem about the person. The first word of each line should begin with a letter from the person's name.
5. Make changes until your poem is just right.
6. Write a title for the poem at the top of the page.

Check out the example on the next page.

GRANDMA

Grows pretty flowers

Reads lots of books

Acts silly sometimes

Nuts are her favorite snack

Dances around the house

Makes good cookies

Always has a hug for me

CHAPTER SIX

Poems That Count

It's as easy as 1, 2, 3!

A **cinquain** is a poem of five lines. It doesn't rhyme. There are different kinds of cinquains. We'll write one adding one more word to each line. Line one has one word. Line two has two words. Line three has three words. Can you guess how many words will be on lines four and five?

ACTIVITY

Cinquain

INSTRUCTIONS:
1. Write the name of a person, place, or thing in your notebook.
2. Think of words that describe your choice. Write them below your idea.
3. On a different page, write your cinquain. Remember to write the words on five lines using one more word on each line.
4. Make changes until your poem is just right.
5. Write a title for your poem at the top of the page.

My First Dive

Water ← (1 word)

Far below ← (2 words)

Me up high ← (3 words)

The board is quivering ← (4 words)

I make a big splash ← (5 words)

You've written five poems so far. Do you have more ideas? Keep writing. You'll be a poet before you know it!

Glossary

acrostic (uh-KRAWSS-tik) a poem in which the subject is spelled out by the first letter of each line

cinquain (SING-kane) a poem of five lines that follows a certain form

couplet (KUHP-lit) two lines of poetry that come one after the other and usually rhyme

free verse (FREE VURSS) poetry without set patterns, usually with lines of different lengths that don't rhyme

poems (POH-uhmz) pieces of writing, often with words that rhyme and follow a rhythm

poet (POH-uht) a person who writes poems

rhyme (RIME) have an ending that sounds like the ending of another word or line

rhythm (RI-thuhm) pattern of beats or sounds in a poem

stanza (STAN-zuh) a group of lines that make up part of a poem

For More Information

BOOKS

Freese, Susan M., comp. *Carrots to Cupcakes: Reading, Writing, and Reciting Poems About Food*. Edina, MN: ABDO Publishing Company, 2008.

Loewen, Nancy. *Words, Wit, and Wonder: Writing Your Own Poem*. Minneapolis: Picture Window Books, 2009.

WEB SITES

BBC—Words and Pictures: Poems
www.bbc.co.uk/schools/wordsandpictures/longvow/ poems/fpoem.shtml
Look here for fun poems and activities.

PBS Kids—Fern's Poetry Club
pbskids.org/arthur/games/poetry/what.html
Learn more about different kinds of poems here.

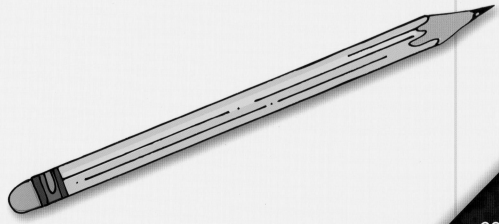

Index

About the Authors

Cecilia Minden, PhD, is the former Director of the Language and Literacy Program at Harvard Graduate School of Education. While at Harvard, Dr. Minden taught several writing courses for teachers. She is now a full-time literacy consultant and the author of more than 100 books for children. Dr. Minden lives in Chapel Hill, North Carolina, with her husband, Dave Cupp, and a cute but spoiled Yorkie named Kenzie.

Kate Roth has a doctorate from Harvard University in Language and Literacy and a masters from Columbia University Teachers College in Curriculum and Teaching. Her work focuses on writing instruction in the primary grades. She has taught first grade, kindergarten, and Reading Recovery. She has also instructed hundreds of teachers from around the world in early literacy practices. She lives in Shanghai, China, with her husband and three children, ages 2, 6, and 9. They do a lot of writing to stay in touch with friends and family and record their experiences.